BE HUMAN KIND

ICE HOUSE BOOKS

Published by Ice House Books

Copyright © 2020 Ice House Books

Compiled by Zulekhá Afzal
Designed and illustrated by Emily Curtis

Ice House Books is an imprint of Half Moon Bay Limited
The Ice House, 124 Walcot Street, Bath, BA1 5BG
www.icehousebooks.co.uk

ISBN 978-1-912867-80-6

Printed in China

TO:

FROM:

YOU CAN ALWAYS GIVE SOMETHING, EVEN IF IT IS ONLY KINDNESS.

ANNE FRANK

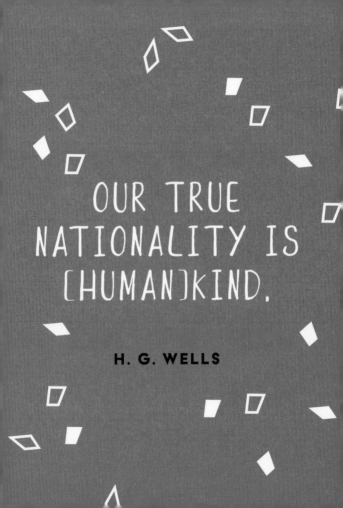

OUR TRUE
NATIONALITY IS
[HUMAN]KIND.

H. G. WELLS

WE MUST
ALLOW
DIFFERENCE
OF TASTE.

JANE AUSTEN,
SENSE AND SENSIBILITY

First keep peace within yourself, then you can also bring peace to others.

THOMAS À KEMPIS

BEFORE GOD,
WE ARE ALL
EQUALLY WISE,
AND EQUALLY
FOOLISH.

ALBERT EINSTEIN

ACTS OF
KINDNESS WILL
ALWAYS BE
REMEMBERED.

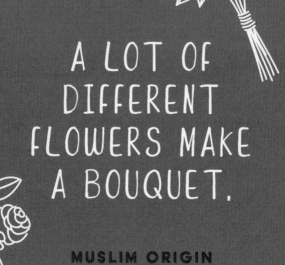

A LOT OF DIFFERENT FLOWERS MAKE A BOUQUET.

MUSLIM ORIGIN

Always be a little kinder than is necessary.

J. M. BARRIE

THE EARTH IS
THE MOTHER OF
ALL PEOPLE,
AND ALL PEOPLE
SHOULD HAVE
EQUAL RIGHTS
UPON IT.

CHIEF JOSEPH

NEVER DISCOURAGE
ANYONE WHO
CONTINUALLY MAKES
PROGRESS, NO
MATTER HOW SLOW.

PLATO

KINDNESS
HEALS THE
DEEPEST
OF WOUNDS.

Compassion will cure more sins than condemnation.

HENRY WARD BEECHER

GIVE WHAT
YOU HAVE.
TO SOMEONE,
IT MAY BE
BETTER THAN
YOU DARE
TO THINK.

**HENRY WADSWORTH
LONGFELLOW**

A SINGLE ACT OF KINDNESS THROWS OUT ROOTS IN ALL DIRECTIONS, AND THE ROOTS SPRING UP AND MAKE NEW TREES.

AMELIA EARHART

IF YOU WANT
TO LIFT YOURSELF
UP, LIFT UP
SOMEONE ELSE.

BOOKER T. WASHINGTON

Celebrate what makes us different.

THERE ARE
TWO WAYS OF
SPREADING LIGHT:
TO BE THE CANDLE
OR THE MIRROR
THAT REFLECTS IT.

EDITH WHARTON

EQUALITY IS THE
SOUL OF LIBERTY;
THERE IS, IN
FACT, NO LIBERTY
WITHOUT IT.

FRANCES WRIGHT

So powerful is the light of unity that it can illuminate the whole earth.

BAHÁ'U'LLÁH

KEEP LOVE IN YOUR
HEART. A LIFE
WITHOUT IT IS LIKE
A SUNLESS GARDEN
WHEN THE FLOWERS
ARE DEAD.

OSCAR WILDE

IN A GENTLE
WAY, YOU CAN
SHAKE THE
WORLD.

MAHATMA GANDHI

UNITY IS STRENGTH, DIVISION IS WEAKNESS.

SWAHILI PROVERB

Individually, we are one drop. Together, we are an ocean.

RYUNOSUKE SATORO

SHARE YOUR SMILE
WITH STRANGERS ...
YOU DON'T KNOW
WHOSE DAY YOU
COULD BRIGHTEN.

One who knows how to show and to accept kindness will be a friend better than any possession.

SOPHOCLES

WHERE THERE
IS UNITY THERE
IS ALWAYS
VICTORY.

PUBLILIUS SYRUS

*I can see myself
in all things
and all people
around me.*

SANSKRIT PHRASE

EACH OF US MUST
WORK FOR [OUR] OWN
IMPROVEMENT, AND
AT THE SAME TIME
SHARE A GENERAL
RESPONSIBILITY FOR
ALL HUMANITY.

MARIE CURIE

THE HAPPINESS
OF LIFE IS MADE UP
OF MINUTE FRACTIONS —
THE LITTLE,
SOON-FORGOTTEN
CHARITIES OF A KISS
OR A SMILE, A KIND
LOOK OR HEARTFELT
COMPLIMENT.

SAMUEL TAYLOR
COLERIDGE

Politeness is the flower of humanity.

JOSEPH JOUBERT

IF YOU HAVE TO
CHOOSE BETWEEN
BEING KIND AND
BEING RIGHT,
CHOOSE BEING
KIND AND YOU WILL
ALWAYS BE RIGHT.

BENEVOLENCE
IS THE
CHARACTERISTIC
ELEMENT OF
HUMANITY.

CONFUCIUS

SOCIETY IS UNITY IN DIVERSITY.

GEORGE HERBERT MEAD

For the strength of the Pack is the Wolf, and the strength of the Wolf is the Pack.

RUDYARD KIPLING,
THE JUNGLE BOOK

UNITY,
NOT UNIFORMITY,
MUST BE OUR AIM.
WE ATTAIN UNITY
ONLY THROUGH
VARIETY.
DIFFERENCES MUST
BE INTEGRATED,
NOT ANNIHILATED,
NOT ABSORBED.

MARY PARKER FOLLETT

BRINGING OUT
THE BEST IN
OTHERS WILL
ALSO BRING OUT
THE BEST IN
YOURSELF.

RISE ABOVE
SECTIONAL INTERESTS
AND PRIVATE
AMBITIONS ... PASS FROM
MATTER TO SPIRIT.
MATTER IS DIVERSITY;
SPIRIT IS LIGHT,
LIFE AND UNITY.

MUHAMMAD IQBAL

Kind words do not cost much. Yet they accomplish much.

BLAISE PASCAL

PLANT LOVE AND
KINDNESS WITH
YOUR WORDS.

HARMONY MAKES SMALL THINGS GROW, LACK OF IT MAKES GREAT THINGS DECAY.

SALLUST

KINDNESS IS THE LANGUAGE WHICH THE DEAF CAN HEAR AND THE BLIND CAN SEE.

MARK TWAIN

All differences in this world are of degree, and not of kind, because oneness is the secret of everything.

SWAMI VIVEKANANDA

IN UNION THERE IS STRENGTH.

AESOP

IT WAS ONLY A
SUNNY SMILE,
AND LITTLE IT COST
IN THE GIVING,
BUT LIKE MORNING
LIGHT IT SCATTERED
THE NIGHT AND
MADE THE DAY
WORTH LIVING.

F. SCOTT FITZGERALD

WHEN YOU
CAN'T FIND THE
SUNSHINE, BE
THE SUNSHINE.

The sole meaning of life is to serve humanity.

LEO TOLSTOY

WE RISE
BY LIFTING
OTHERS.

ROBERT G. INGERSOLL

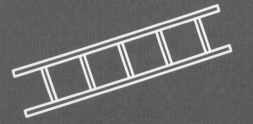

TO SPEAK KINDLY
DOES NOT HURT
THE TONGUE.

PROVERB

GOOD NATURE WILL
ALWAYS SUPPLY THE
ABSENCE OF BEAUTY;
BUT BEAUTY CANNOT
SUPPLY THE ABSENCE
OF GOOD NATURE.

JOSEPH ADDISON

Be as kind to
yourself as you
are to others.

WHAT WISDOM CAN YOU FIND THAT IS GREATER THAN KINDNESS?

JEAN-JACQUES ROUSSEAU

KINDNESS IS THE
LIGHT THAT
DISSOLVES ALL
WALLS BETWEEN
SOULS, FAMILIES,
AND NATIONS.

PARAMAHANSA YOGANANDA

DARKNESS
CANNOT DRIVE
OUT DARKNESS;
ONLY LIGHT
CAN DO THAT.

MARTIN LUTHER KING JR

In a world where you can be anything, be kind.

EVERYONE IS
KNEADED OUT
OF THE SAME
DOUGH BUT NOT
BAKED IN THE
SAME OVEN.

YIDDISH PROVERB

FRIENDS SHOW
THEIR LOVE
IN TIMES OF
TROUBLE, NOT
IN HAPPINESS.

EURIPIDES

WE'RE ALL
PART OF THE
TAPESTRY
THAT IS LIFE.

Compassion is the basis of morality.

ARTHUR SCHOPENHAUER

WE SHOULD GIVE AS
WE WOULD RECEIVE,
CHEERFULLY, QUICKLY,
AND WITHOUT
HESITATION; FOR THERE
IS NO GRACE IN A
BENEFIT THAT STICKS
TO THE FINGERS.

LUCIUS ANNAEUS SENECA

UNITY AND
DIVERSITY STAND
HAND IN HAND.

GENTLENESS
AND KINDNESS
WILL MAKE
OUR HOMES A
PARADISE
UPON EARTH.

C. A. BARTOL

Peace and friendship with all [human]kind is our wisest policy, and I wish we may be permitted to pursue it.

THOMAS JEFFERSON

LIFE WITHOUT LOVE IS LIKE A TREE WITHOUT BLOSSOMS OR FRUIT.

KAHLIL GIBRAN

CHOOSE LOVE
AND KINDNESS,
ALWAYS.

REAL GENEROSITY
IS DOING SOMETHING
NICE FOR SOMEONE
WHO WILL
NEVER FIND OUT.

FRANK A. CLARK

We are members one of another; so that you cannot injure or help your neighbour without injuring or helping yourself.

GEORGE BERNARD SHAW

HUMANITY HAS ONLY SCRATCHED THE SURFACE OF ITS REAL POTENTIAL.

PEACE PILGRIM

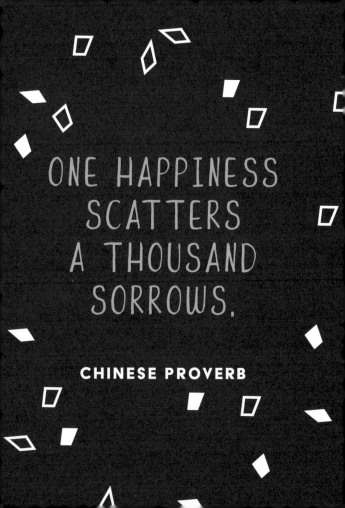

ONE HAPPINESS
SCATTERS
A THOUSAND
SORROWS.

CHINESE PROVERB

NEVER GIVE UP
ON EACH OTHER.

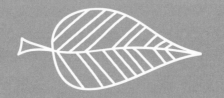

We are the leaves
of one branch,
the drops of
one sea, the flowers
of one garden.

**JEAN-BAPTISTE HENRI
LACORDAIRE**

EMPATHY IS
SEEING WITH THE
EYES OF ANOTHER,
LISTENING WITH
THE EARS OF
ANOTHER AND
FEELING WITH THE
HEART OF ANOTHER.

ALFRED ADLER

DIVERSITY IS
WHAT MAKES OUR
PLANET SPECIAL.

FIND THE
SWEETNESS IN
YOUR OWN HEART,
THEN YOU MAY FIND
THE SWEETNESS
IN EVERY HEART.

RUMI

Remember upon the conduct of each depends the fate of all.

ALEXANDER THE GREAT

LOVE.
KINDNESS.
COMPASSION.

THE INGREDIENTS
FOR LIFE ARE
SIMPLE.

PEACE CANNOT
BE KEPT
BY FORCE;
IT CAN ONLY BE
ACHIEVED BY
UNDERSTANDING.

ALBERT EINSTEIN

IF EVERYONE IS
MOVING FORWARD
TOGETHER, THEN
SUCCESS TAKES
CARE OF ITSELF.

HENRY FORD

We are all alike,
on the inside.

MARK TWAIN

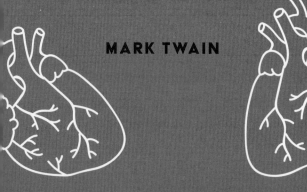

A LITTLE KINDNESS
CAN CHANGE NOT
ONLY SOMEONE
ELSE'S DAY, BUT
YOUR DAY TOO.

BE THE CHANGE
YOU WISH
TO SEE IN
THE WORLD.

MAHATMA GANDHI

NO ACT OF
KINDNESS,
NO MATTER HOW
SMALL, IS
EVER WASTED.

AESOP

*If you want
to go fast,
go alone.
If you want
to go far,
go together.*

AFRICAN PROVERB

CONSTANT
KINDNESS CAN
ACCOMPLISH MUCH.
AS THE SUN
MAKES ICE MELT,
KINDNESS CAUSES
MISUNDERSTANDING,
MISTRUST AND
HOSTILITY TO
EVAPORATE.

ALBERT SCHWEITZER

LET YOUR
DIFFERENCES SHINE
IN EVERYTHING
YOU DO.

MY COUNTRY
IS THE
WORLD; MY
[COMPATRIOTS]
ARE ALL
[HUMAN]KIND.

WILLIAM LLOYD GARRISON

I feel that there is nothing more truly artistic than to love people.

VINCENT VAN GOGH

OUR DIFFERENCES
ARE WHAT MAKE
US SO MUCH
STRONGER
WHEN WE STAND
TOGETHER.

IT IS IN
THE SHELTER
OF EACH OTHER
THAT THE
PEOPLE LIVE.

IRISH PROVERB

THE
SIGNIFICANCE
WHICH IS
IN UNITY IS
AN ETERNAL
WONDER.

RABINDRANETH TAGORE

Kind words can be short and easy to speak but their echoes are truly endless.

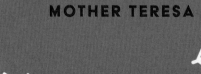

MOTHER TERESA

WHEN YOU SHOW KINDNESS, IT SPREADS FURTHER THAN YOU CAN SEE.

MY COUNTRY IS
THE WORLD, AND
MY RELIGION IS
TO DO GOOD.

THOMAS PAINE

LET'S HELP
EACH OTHER
BLOOM.

Act with kindness, but do not expect gratitude.

CONFUCIUS

WHOEVER IS HAPPY WILL MAKE OTHERS HAPPY.

ANNE FRANK

LIFE IS SO
MUCH SIMPLER
WHEN WE DO IT
TOGETHER.

THE GREATEST
GOOD YOU CAN DO
FOR ANOTHER IS
NOT JUST TO SHARE
YOUR RICHES BUT
TO REVEAL TO
[THEM THEIR] OWN.

BENJAMIN DISRAELI

Kindness isn't
a difficult
language to learn.

LIFE ETCHES ITSELF ONTO OUR FACES AS WE GROW OLDER, SHOWING OUR VIOLENCE, EXCESSES OR KINDNESS.

REMBRANDT

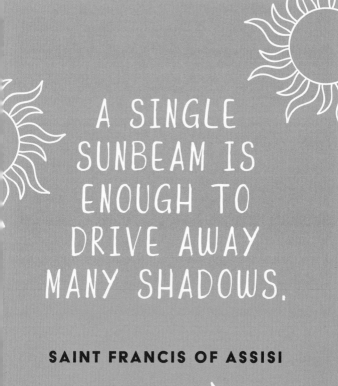

A SINGLE
SUNBEAM IS
ENOUGH TO
DRIVE AWAY
MANY SHADOWS.

SAINT FRANCIS OF ASSISI

HOW BEAUTIFUL
A DAY CAN BE,
WHEN KINDNESS
TOUCHES IT!

GEORGE ELLISTON

*A warm smile
is the universal
language
of kindness.*

WILLIAM ARTHUR WARD

HOW FAR THAT
LITTLE CANDLE
THROWS [ITS] BEAMS!
SO SHINES A
GOOD DEED IN
A WEARY WORLD.

WILLIAM SHAKESPEARE,
THE MERCHANT OF VENICE

KINDNESS IS
INFECTIOUS.

ALL THE
CITIZENS OF
A STATE CANNOT
BE EQUALLY
POWERFUL,
BUT THEY MAY
BE EQUALLY FREE.

VOLTAIRE

Generosity is the flower of justice.

NATHANIEL HAWTHORNE

A LITTLE
COMPASSION
CAN BRIGHTEN
UP THE
DARKEST DAY.

DELIBERATELY
SEEK
OPPORTUNITIES
FOR KINDNESS,
SYMPATHY,
AND PATIENCE.

EVELYN UNDERHILL

WE LOOK FORWARD
TO THE TIME WHEN
THE POWER OF LOVE
WILL REPLACE THE
LOVE OF POWER.
THEN WILL OUR
WORLD KNOW THE
BLESSINGS OF PEACE.

WILLIAM EWART GLADSTONE

Throw
kindness around
like confetti.

YOU CANNOT DO A KINDNESS TOO SOON, FOR YOU NEVER KNOW HOW SOON IT WILL BE TOO LATE.

RALPH WALDO EMERSON

A PART OF
KINDNESS
CONSISTS IN
LOVING PEOPLE
MORE THAN
THEY DESERVE.

JOSEPH JOUBERT

A KIND WORD
IS LIKE A
SPRING DAY.

RUSSIAN PROVERB

*The love we
give away is the
only love we keep.*

ELBERT HUBBARD

TRY TO BE
A RAINBOW
IN SOMEONE'S
CLOUD.

MAYA ANGELOU

KINDNESS
GIVES
BIRTH TO
KINDNESS.

SOPHOCLES

THIS IS MY CREED;
HAPPINESS IS
THE ONLY GOOD;
REASON THE ONLY
TORCH; JUSTICE
THE ONLY WORSHIP,
HUMANITY THE ONLY
RELIGION, AND LOVE
THE ONLY PRIEST.

ROBERT G. INGERSOLL

Instead of putting others in their place, put yourself in their place.

AMISH PROVERB

COLOUR IN THE
WORLD AND
ALL WILL BE
BRIGHTER.

THE MOST
WORTH-WHILE
THING IS TO TRY
TO PUT HAPPINESS
INTO THE LIVES
OF OTHERS.

ROBERT BADEN-POWELL

THE EARTH
IS BUT ONE
COUNTRY AND
[HUMAN]KIND
ITS CITIZENS.

BAHÁ'U'LLÁH

You can accomplish by kindness what you cannot by force.

PUBLILIUS SYRUS

THE MORE ONE JUDGES, THE LESS ONE LOVES.

HONORÉ DE BALZAC

BEING KIND
WILL NEVER
GO OUT OF
FASHION.

THE DAY HUNGER
DISAPPEARS,
THE WORLD WILL
SEE THE GREATEST
SPIRITUAL EXPLOSION
HUMANITY HAS
EVER SEEN.

FEDERICO GARCÍA LORCA

Whenever there is a human being, there is an opportunity for kindness.

LUCIUS ANNAEUS SENECA

KINDNESS IS
IN OUR POWER,
EVEN WHEN
FONDNESS
IS NOT.

SAMUEL JOHNSON

A KIND ACT
IS AN ACT
OF BEAUTY.

GENTLENESS
IS THE
ANTIDOTE
FOR CRUELTY.

PHAEDRUS

A laugh, to be joyous, must flow from a joyous heart, for without kindness, there can be no true joy.

THOMAS CARLYLE

THE TRUEST
GREATNESS LIES
IN BEING KIND,
THE TRUEST
WISDOM IN A
HAPPY MIND.

ELLA WHEELER WILCOX

THE MOST
POWERFUL SYMPTOM
OF LOVE IS A
TENDERNESS
WHICH BECOMES
AT TIMES ALMOST
INSUPPORTABLE.

VICTOR HUGO

KINDNESS MAKES
A [PERSON] FEEL
GOOD WHETHER
IT'S BEING DONE
TO [THEM] OR
BY [THEM].

FRANK A. CLARK

Tenderness and kindness are not signs of weakness and despair, but manifestations of strength and resolution.

KAHLIL GIBRAN

NEVER GIVE UP
ON THE POWER
OF KINDNESS.

THREE THINGS IN
HUMAN LIFE ARE
IMPORTANT.
THE FIRST IS
TO BE KIND.
THE SECOND IS
TO BE KIND.
AND THE THIRD
IS TO BE KIND.

HENRY JAMES

ONCE THE
GAME IS OVER,
THE KING AND
THE PAWN GO
BACK IN THE
SAME BOX.

ITALIAN PROVERB

There is no charm equal to tenderness of heart.

JANE AUSTEN,
EMMA

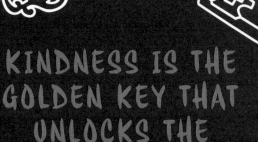

KINDNESS IS THE
GOLDEN KEY THAT
UNLOCKS THE
HEARTS OF OTHERS.

HENRY DRUMMOND

NEVER LOSE
A CHANCE OF
SAYING A
KIND WORD.

**WILLIAM MAKEPEACE
THACKERAY**

I FEEL NO NEED FOR ANY OTHER FAITH THAN MY FAITH IN THE KINDNESS OF HUMAN BEINGS,

PEARL S. BUCK

Kindness makes the load lighter and life brighter.

NOTHING IS
SO STRONG AS
GENTLENESS,
NOTHING SO
GENTLE AS REAL
STRENGTH.

SAINT FRANCIS DE SALES

A LITTLE
THOUGHT AND
A LITTLE KINDNESS
ARE OFTEN WORTH
MORE THAN A GREAT
DEAL OF MONEY.

JOHN RUSKIN

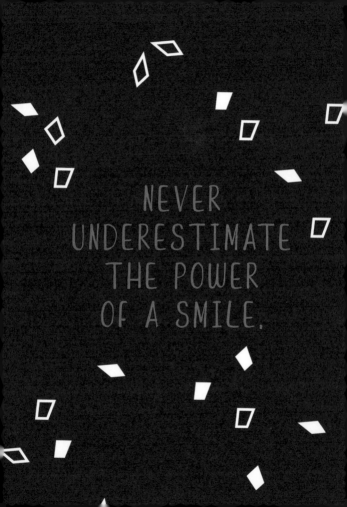

NEVER
UNDERESTIMATE
THE POWER
OF A SMILE.

Friendship is the only cement that will ever hold the world together.

WOODROW WILSON

EVERY ACT
OF KINDNESS
GROWS THE
SPIRIT AND
STRENGTHENS
THE SOUL.

WHAT SUNSHINE
IS TO FLOWERS,
SMILES ARE
TO HUMANITY.
THESE ARE BUT
TRIFLES, TO BE SURE;
BUT SCATTERED ALONG
LIFE'S PATHWAY,
THE GOOD THEY DO
IS INCONCEIVABLE.

JOSEPH ADDISON

THE BEST
PORTION OF A GOOD
[PERSON'S] LIFE:
THEIR LITTLE,
NAMELESS,
UNREMEMBERED,
ACTS OF KINDNESS
AND OF LOVE.

WILLIAM WORDSWORTH,
TINTERN ABBEY

Kindness

is wisdom.

PHILIP JAMES BAILEY

REAL KINDNESS
SEEKS NO RETURN;
WHAT RETURN CAN
THE WORLD MAKE
TO RAIN CLOUDS?

THIRUVALLUVAR

LIFT OTHERS
BEFORE THEY
HAVE A CHANCE
TO FALL.

A SINGLE ARROW
IS EASILY
BROKEN, BUT
NOT TEN IN
A BUNDLE.

JAPANESE PROVERB

Kindness is no virtue, but a common duty.

FREDERICK GREENWOOD

THE SMALLEST
ACT OF KINDNESS
IS WORTH
MORE THAN
THE GRANDEST
INTENTION.

OSCAR WILDE